PARROT
COLORING BOOK

Get FREE printable coloring pages and discounted book prices sent straight to your e-mail inbox every week!

Sign up at:

www.adultcoloringworld.net

ISBN-13: 978-1535566650
ISBN-10: 1535566655

PREVIEWS:

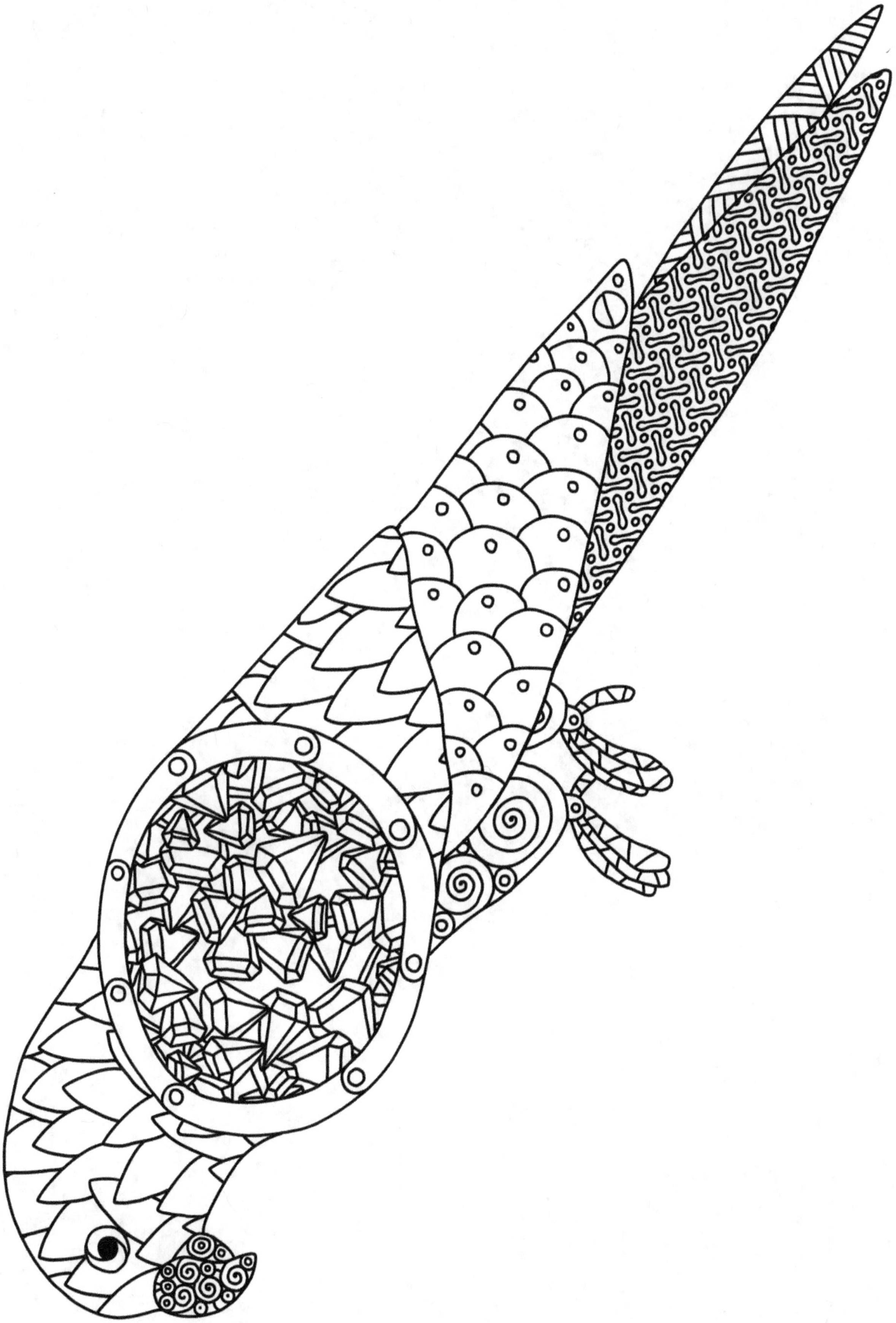

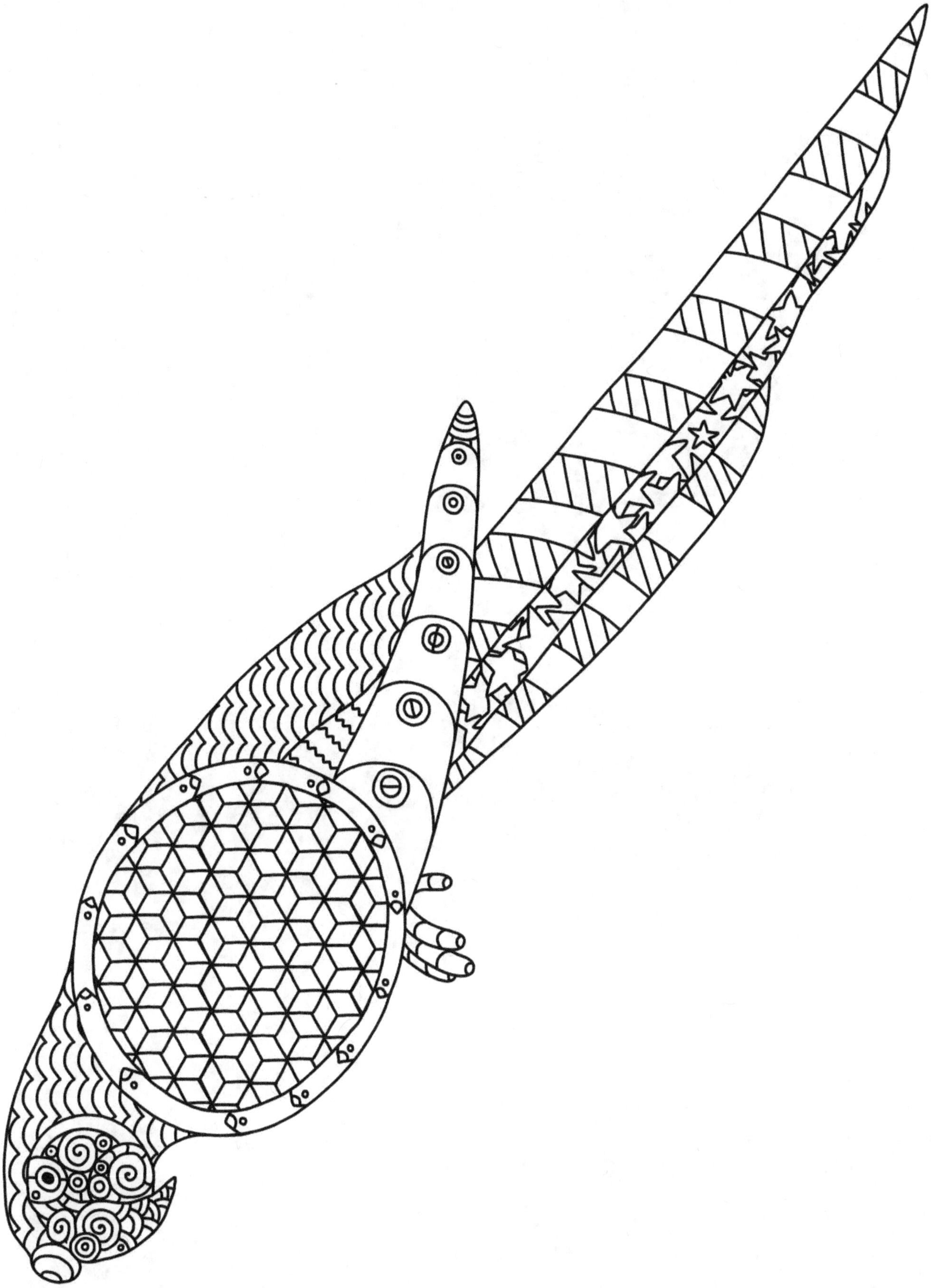

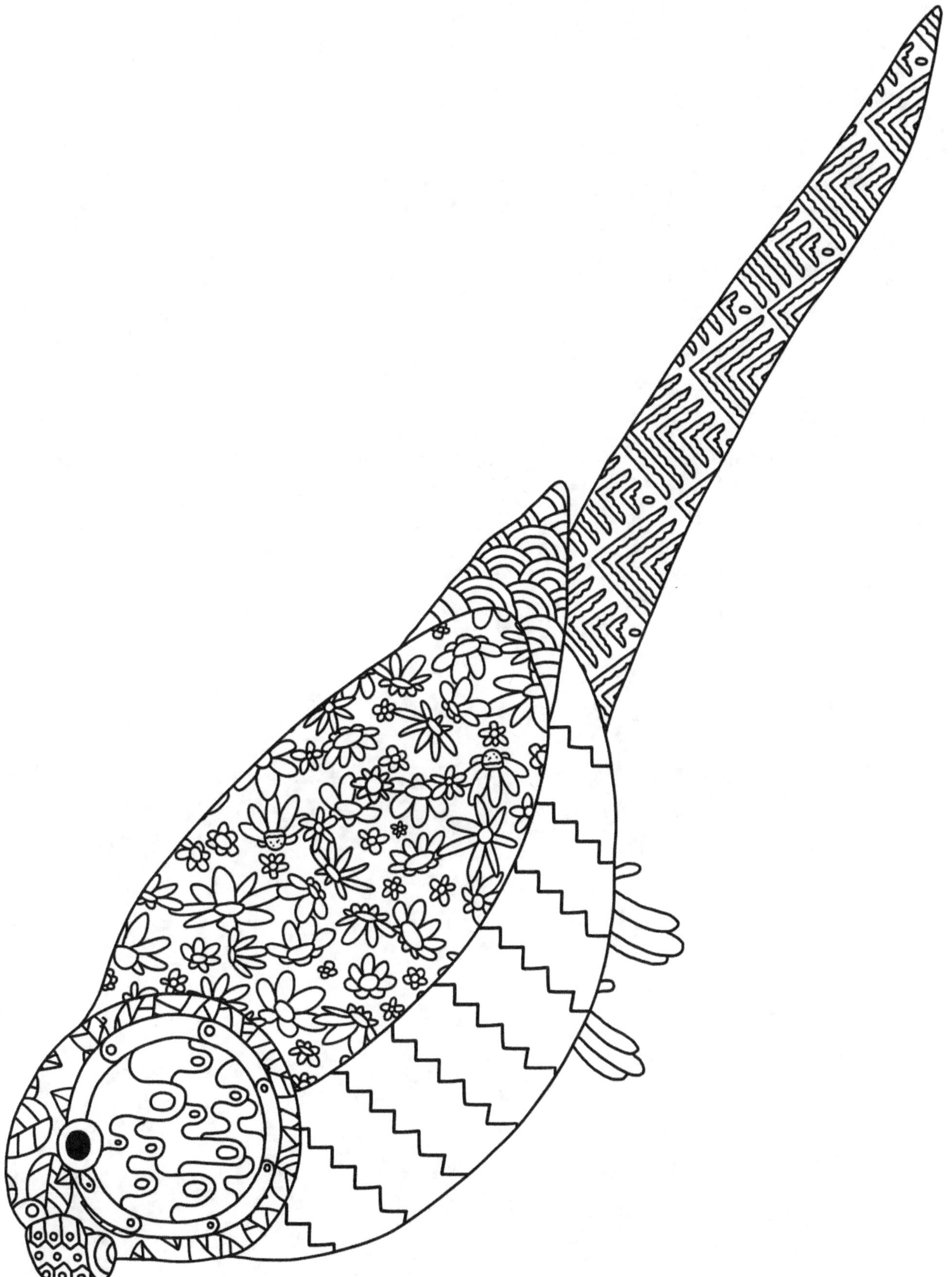

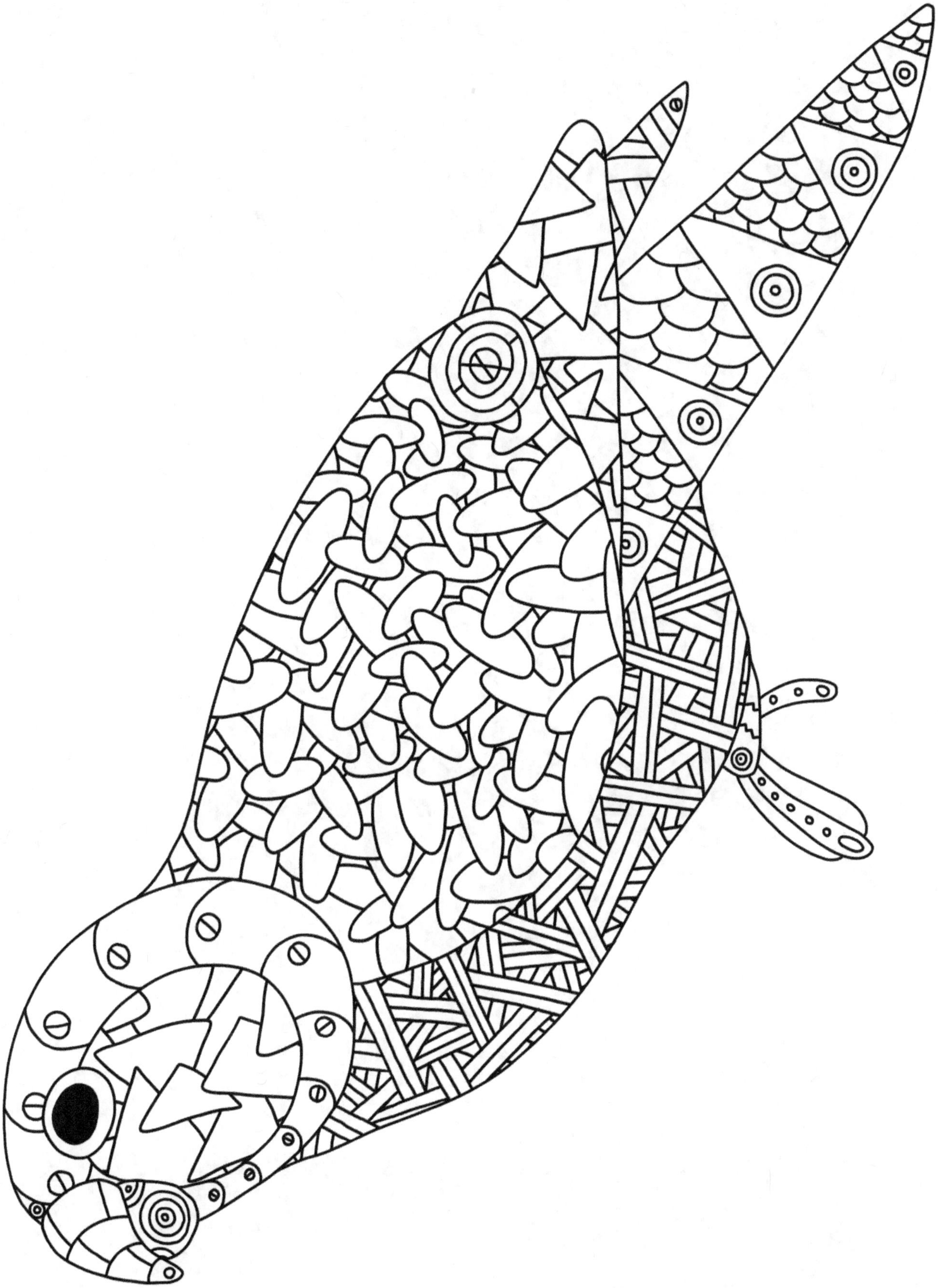

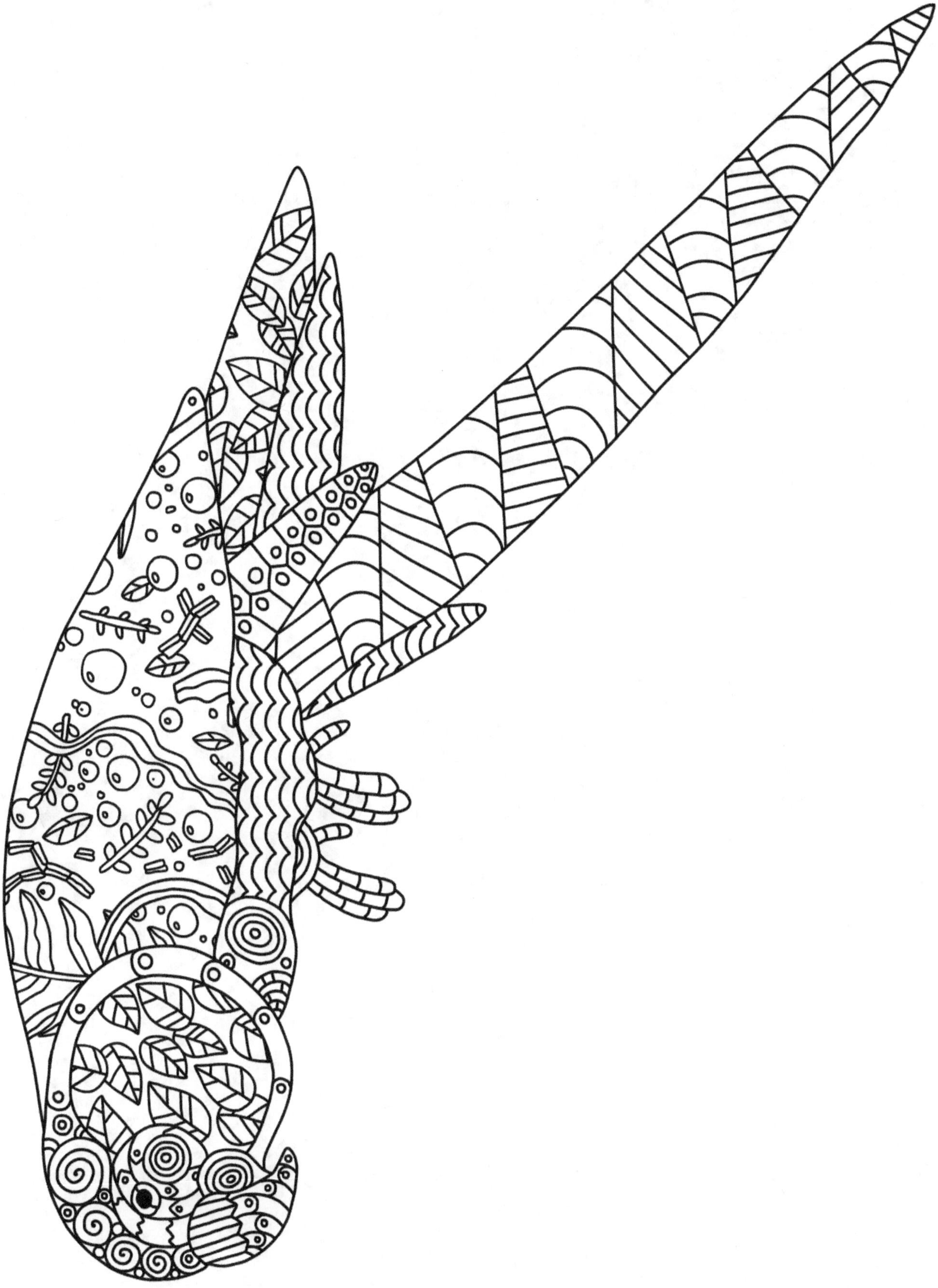

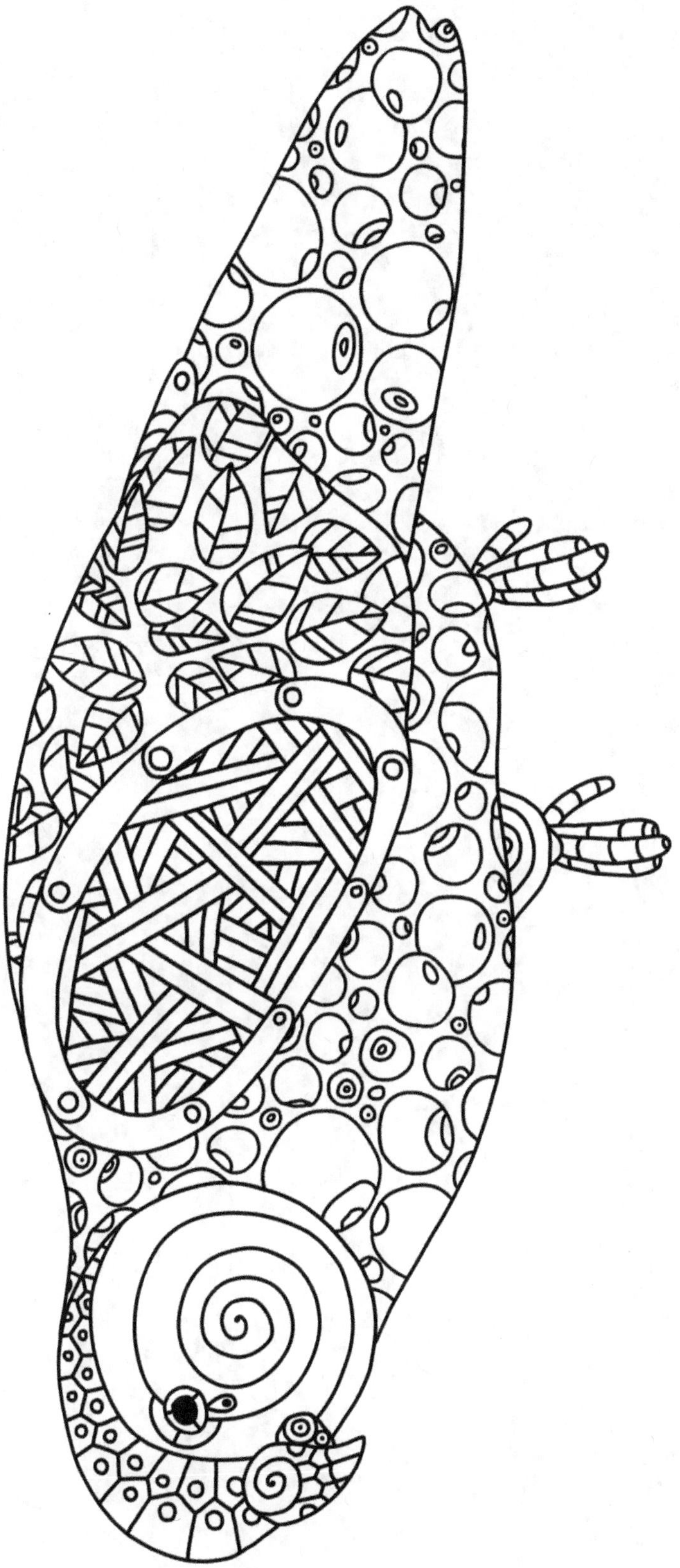

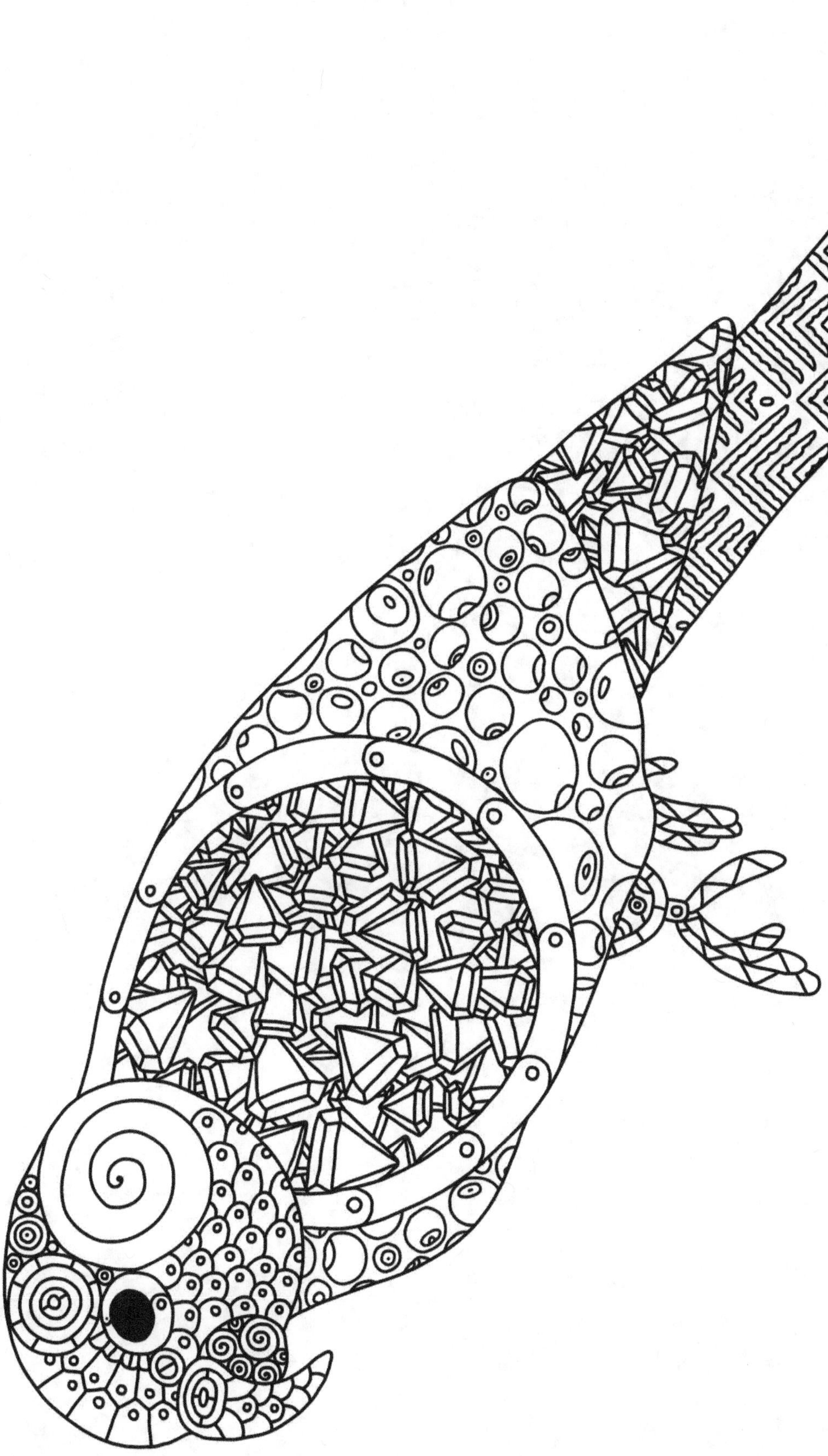

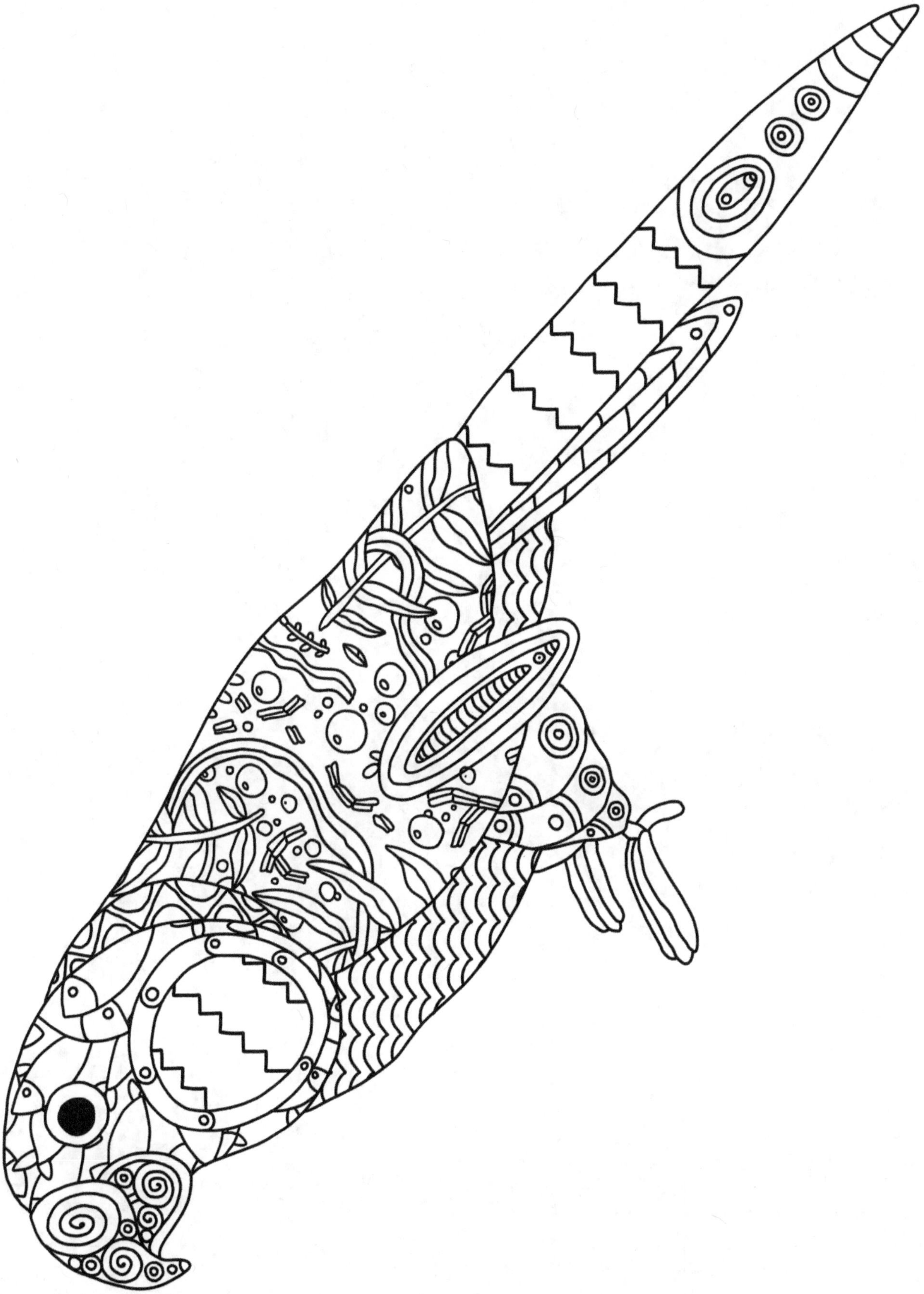

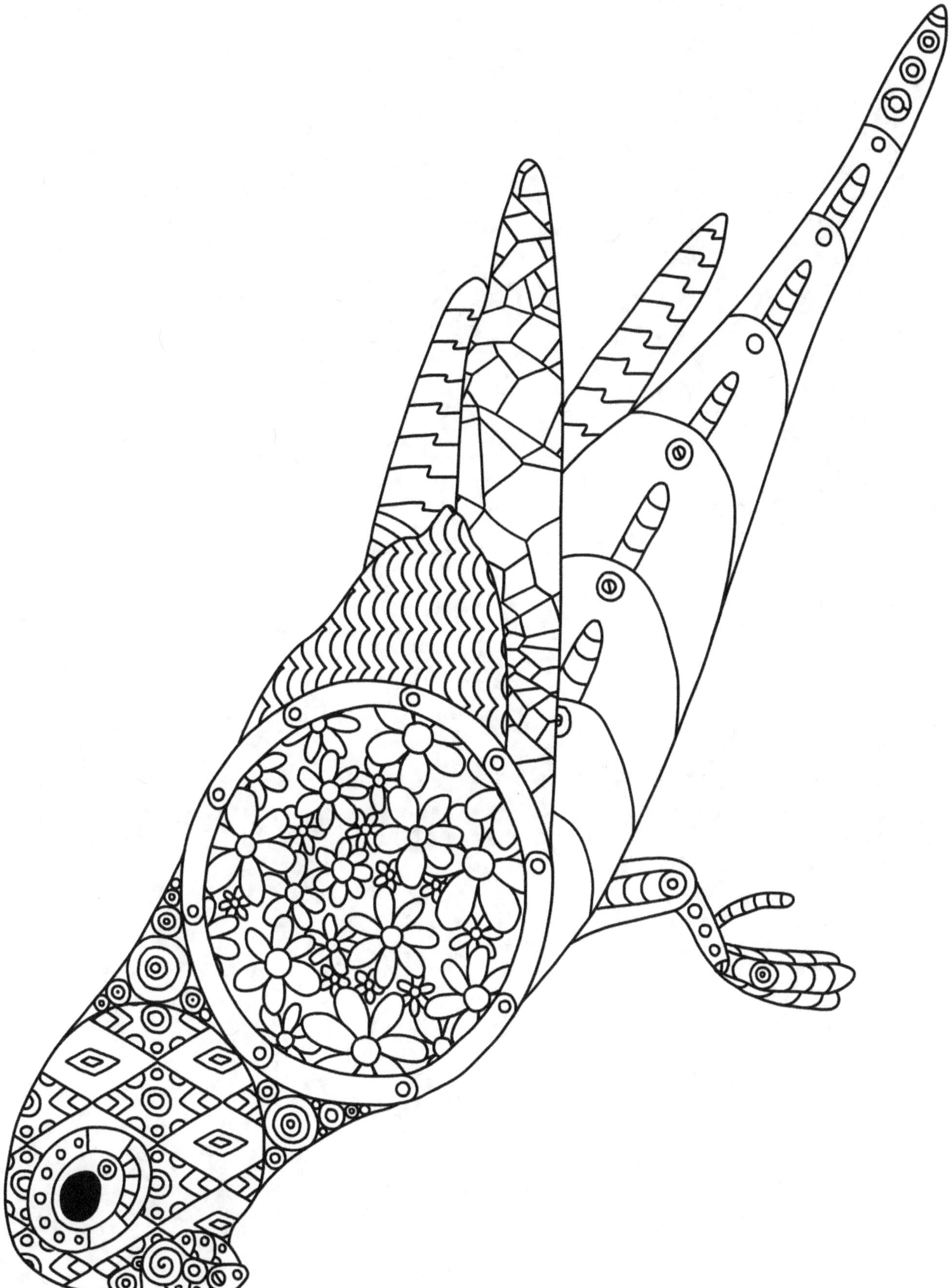

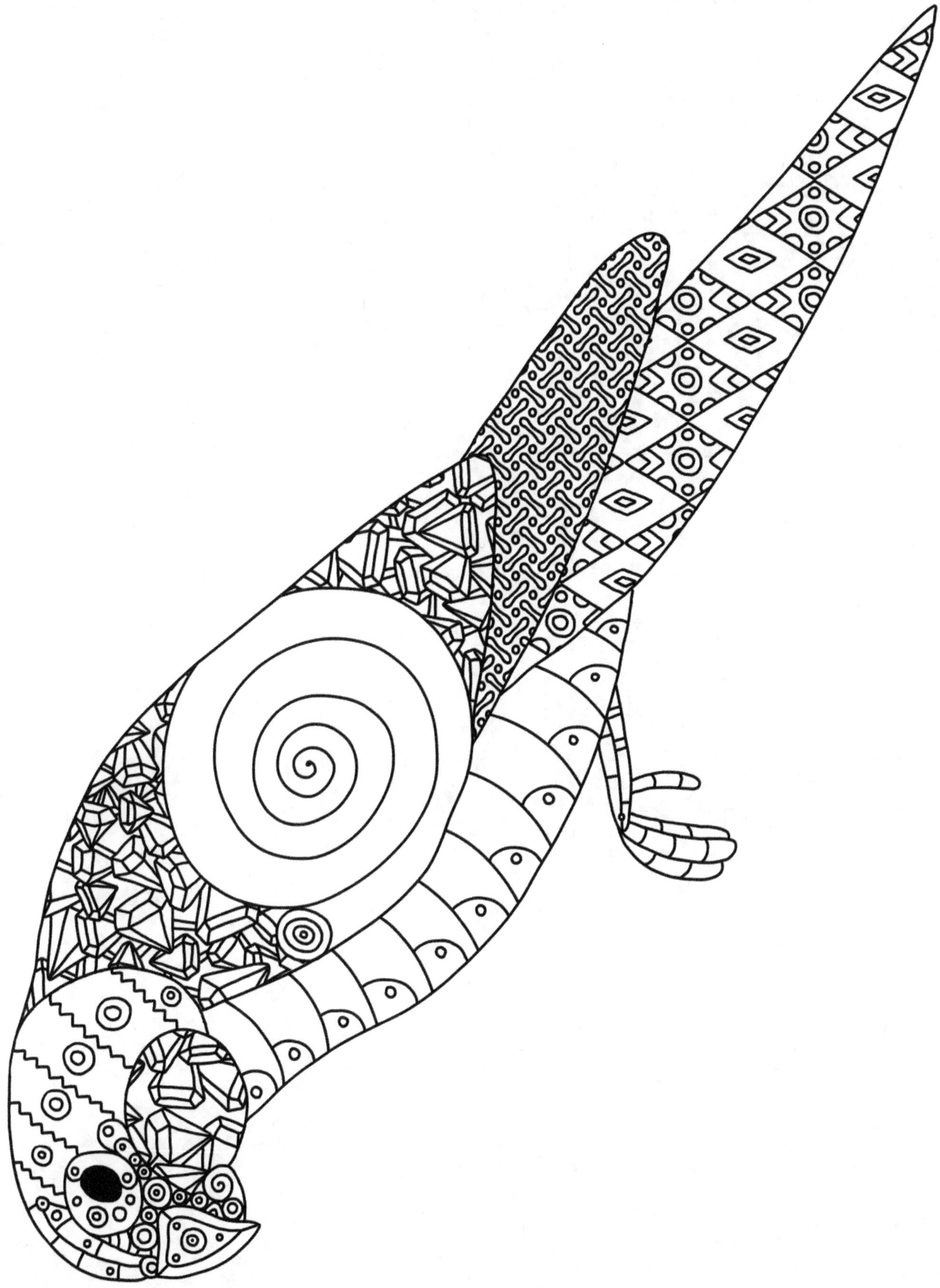

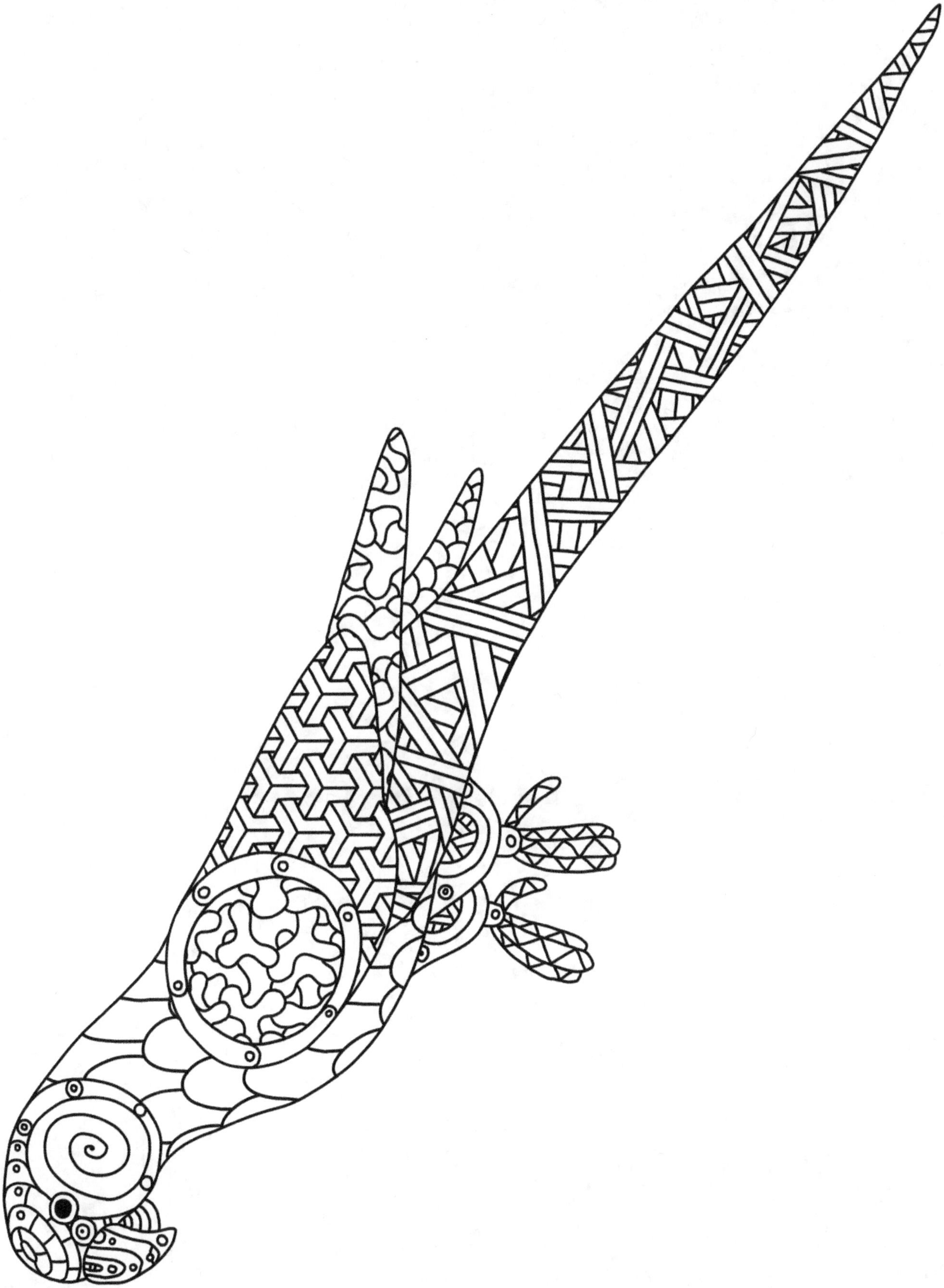

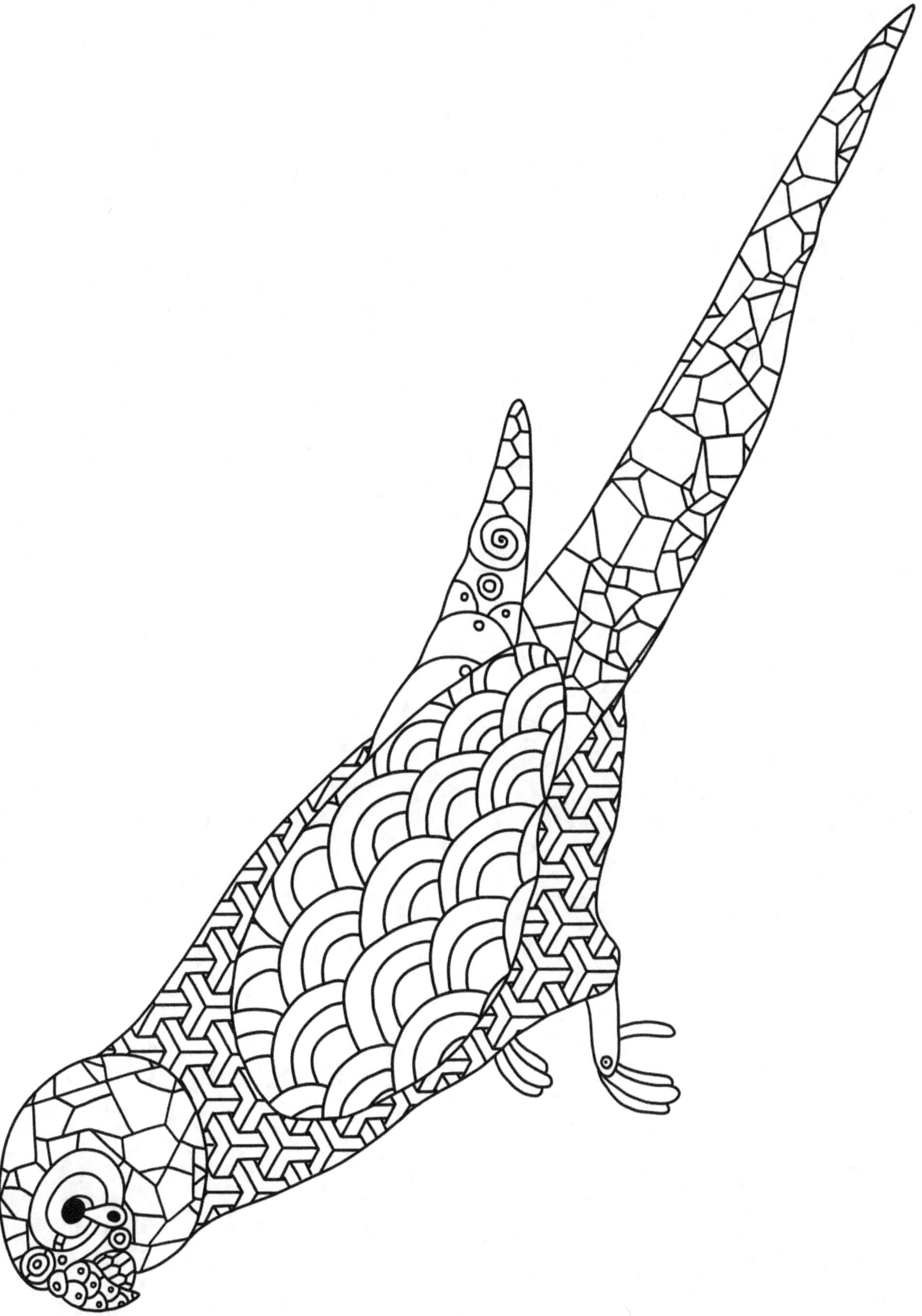

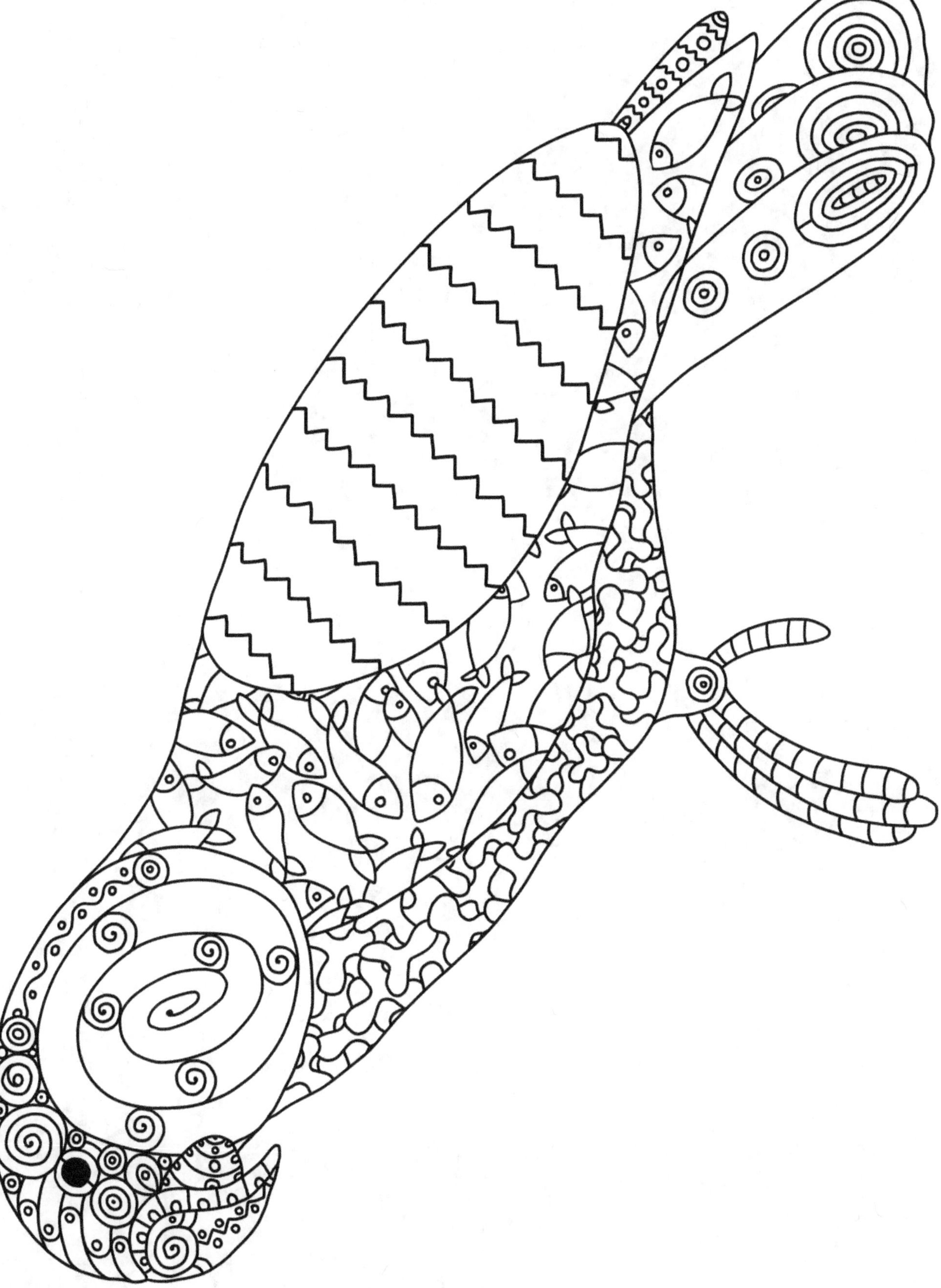

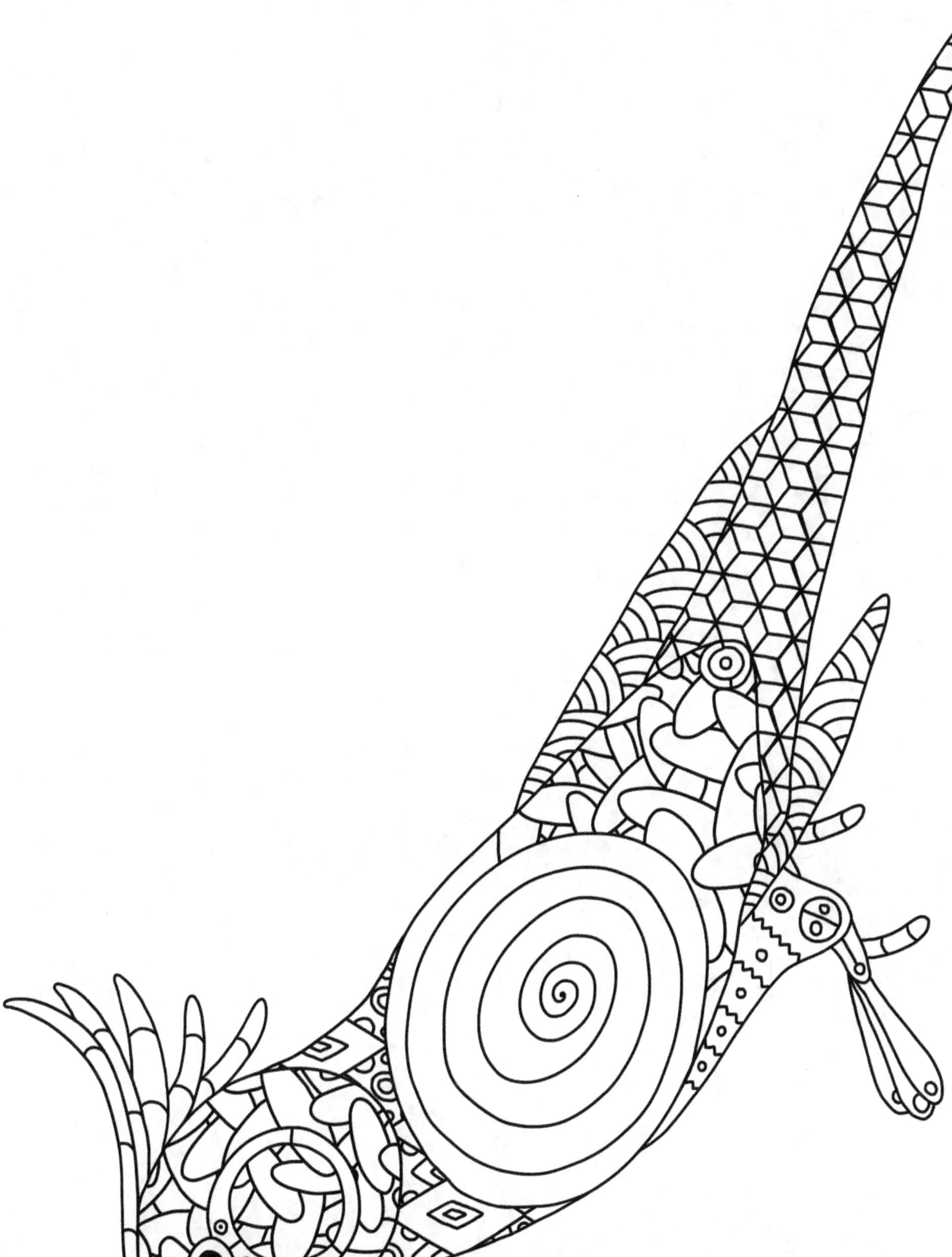

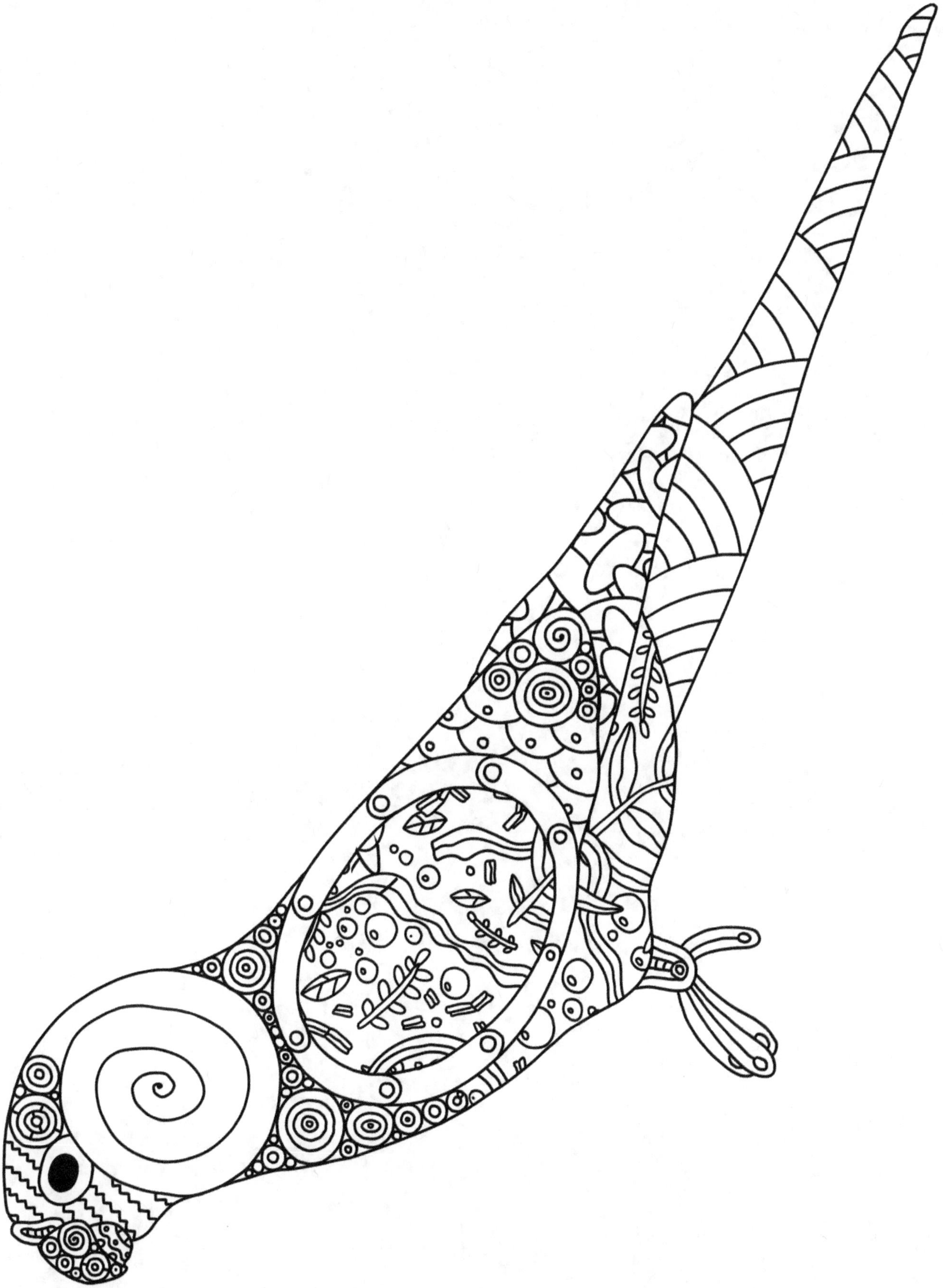

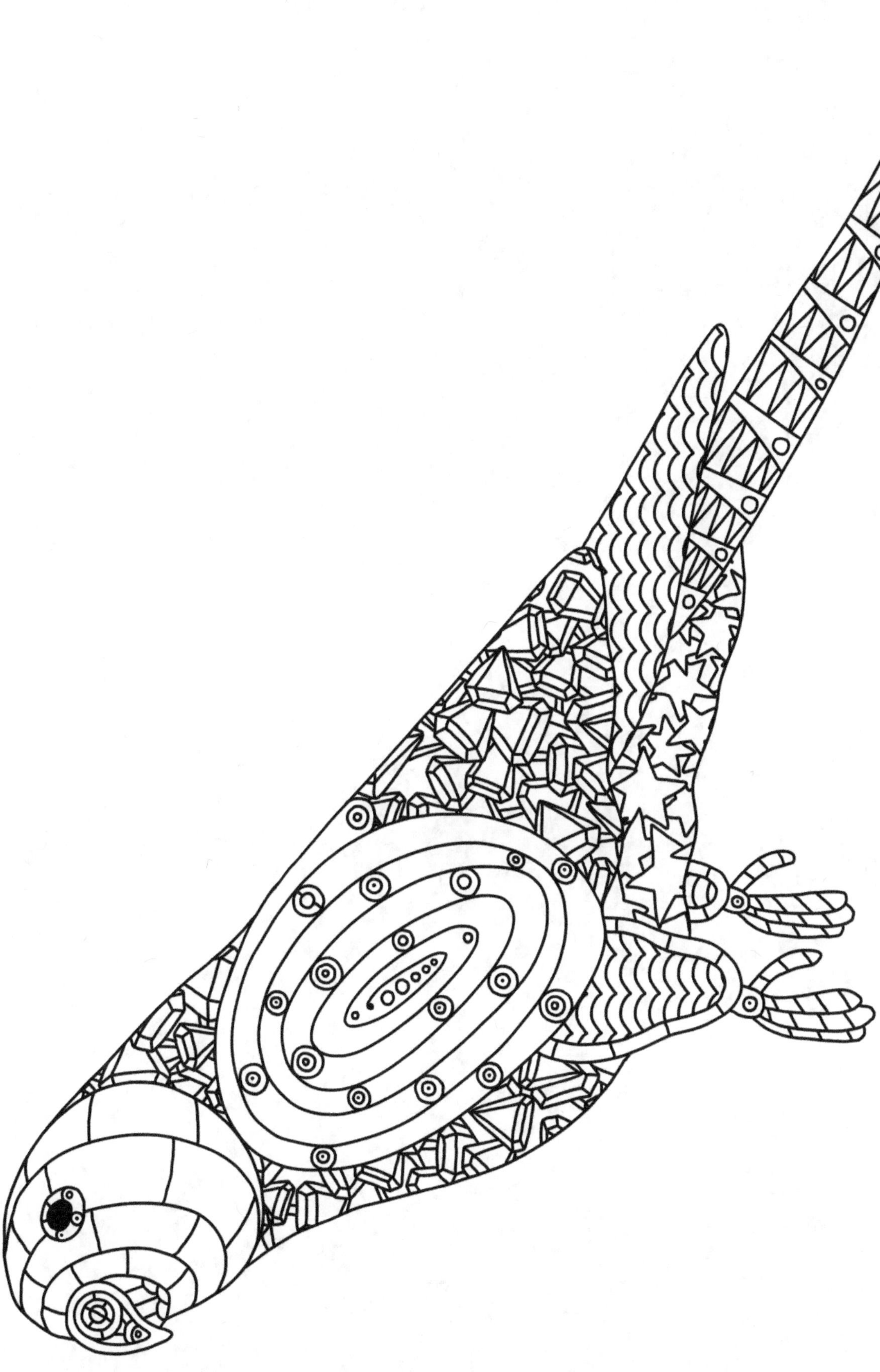

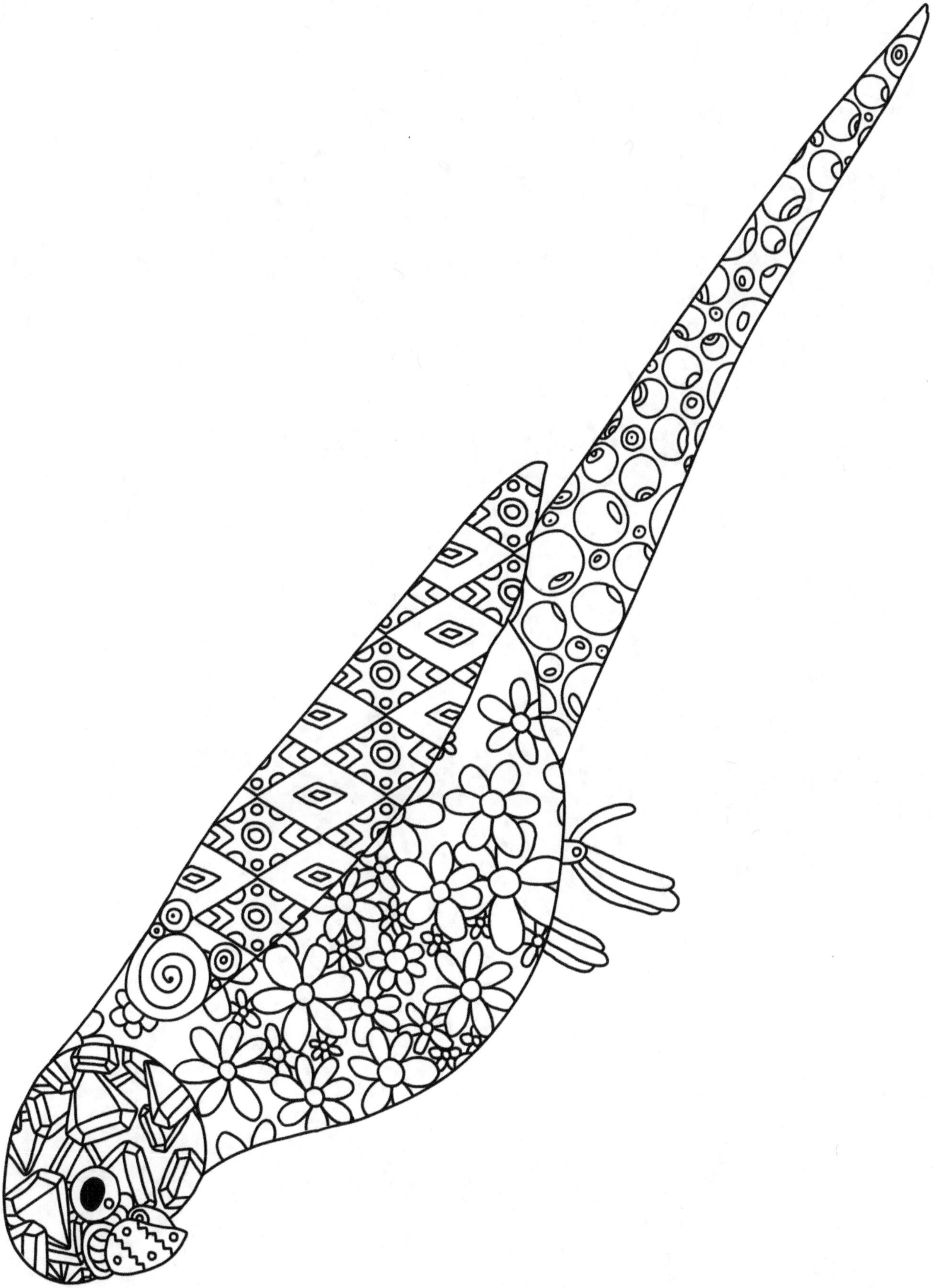

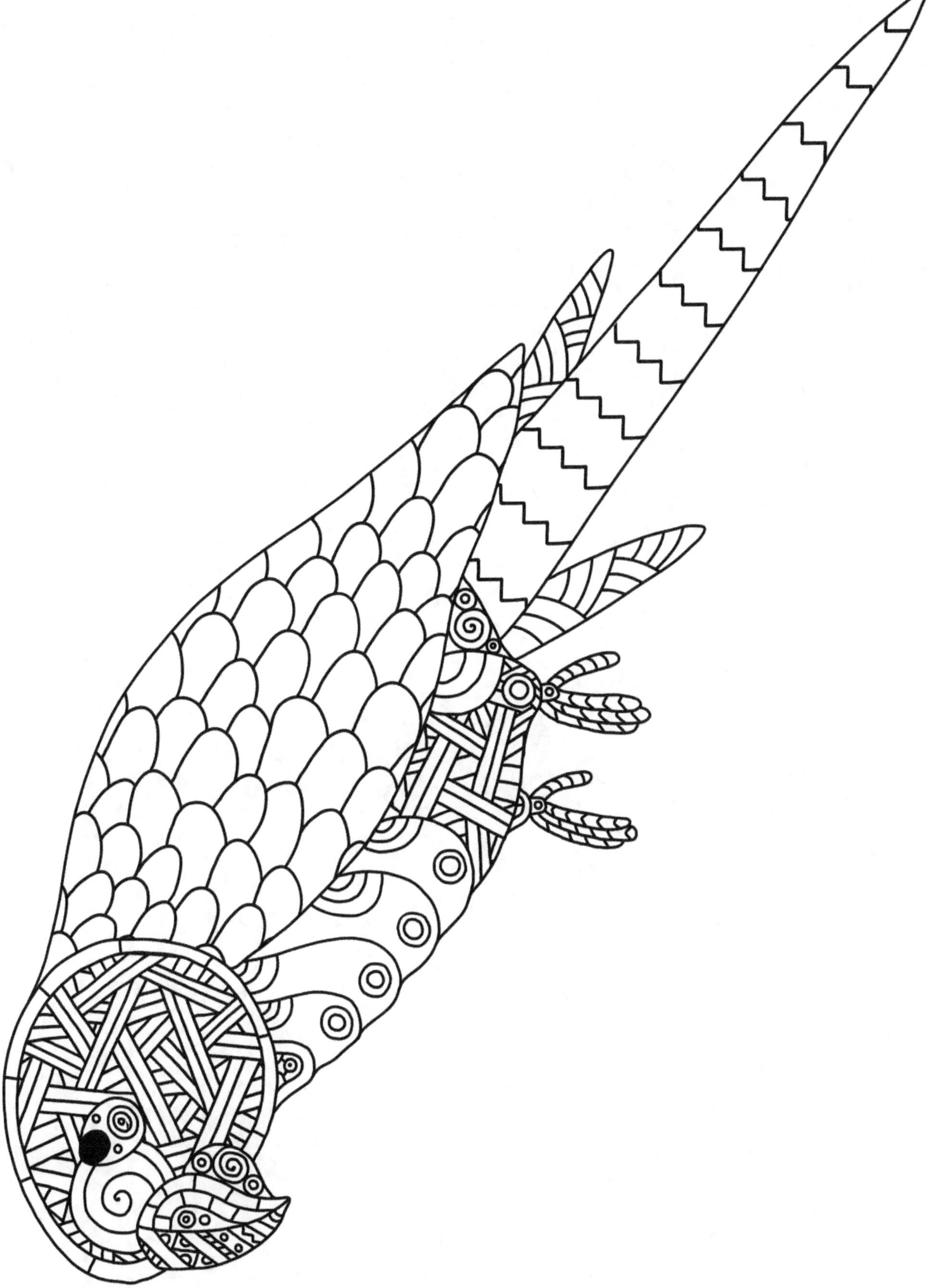

Color Test Page

Color Test Page

www.ingramcontent.com/pod-product-compliance
Lightning Source LLC
Chambersburg PA
CBHW080324290526
45793CB00006B/1200
9781535566650